IN THE MARGINS

IN THE MARGINS

Poetry by

Diane Marquart Moore

Border Press
PO Box 3124
Sewanee, Tennessee 37375
www.borderpressbooks.com
borderpress@gmail.com

ISBN: 978-1-7346802-5-6

Library of Congress Control Number: 2021934709

Cover watercolor by Diane Marquart Moore

Cover design by Victoria Sullivan

Printed in the United States

For Victoria Sullivan

SETTING THE CLOCK

That says it's ten minutes behind
or fifteen or even thirty
on any lazy day.
You say you set it every morning
your idea of keeping time,
but I look to the stove,
face on a white porcelain headboard—
a more reliable time keeper.
The sun comes up,
maybe nothing new comes to light,
morning always a bit late.
You stand at the kitchen window
watching night disappear
waiting for change
on a blue wooden face,
a cheap dime store clock
that doesn't know its proper place.
And how long will it think
everything a matter
of accidental fortune?

IN THE MARGIN

It's better to put things
in the margins,
the place of most importance,
to remember thoughts
illegible, hasty scribbles
that carry the essence
of distilled wisdom
written with a fountain pen
that helps to underline its ancientness
preferably black ink and Parker pen
emphasizing you're in the know
about something that wants to be known,
has made itself certainly philosophical
in a simple brief phrase…
in the margins.

DESERT MEMORIES

If you go too far
into the memory box
you will run into shadows,
places where sun beams
have been harsh,
absent of connection and variance.
The air of too much winter
points you toward barrel cacti,
latticed spines diffusing sun rays,
organ pipes struggling for life…
long stretches without oasis.

ADRIFT

It was just a small green glass
filled with Mescal from the Century plant,
compliments of a bar in Oaxaca, Mexico,
juice from a plant rumored
not to receive an old age pension,
one that blooms once, then dies.
It was a bit stronger than the margaritas
we drank every day in Alpine, Texas,
Triple Sec and tequila, limes,
ice in a bucket, a pocket knife
we found in a hardware store —
the bar tools of desert drinkers.
We ate burritos at a gas station,
a Terlingua recipe that the Mexican woman
had made for hungry field workers.
We were Desperadoes adrift
in Terlingua, Marfa, Oaxaca —
the memories merge
like good times,
and we're too old to live again.
I looked for the jojoba plant
in the hot stretches of desert
because a little jojoba oil goes a long way;
the Mexicans use it to restore hair.
And you never see a bald Mexican.

Highway 41A

An army of 18 wheelers swerves around curves
between Sewanee and Cowan,
increased volume and velocity —
trucks Uncle Ed would have loved:
long beds, high cabs —
transport that I abhor.
They fume Takeover,
pothole makers,
smelly speed lovers,
always making a pass
at sides of highways
or trying to crowd out
safe drivers, outraged passengers,
those who hold up a middle finger
as they pass and descend to the valley,
reach the sprawling stone house,
dirty pond in front for sale —
offering the comfort of leveling off.

GROCERIES FOR TWO WEEKS

Two nervous Chihuahuas dance,
shake the cab of a faded red pickup,
bark furiously at me
where I'm stationed
safe on a front seat
smelling of new leather —
a yellow/green tinted Subaru
nestled among the phalanx of black cars.

A flock of sparrows and I
peck in the Kroger parking lot,
they at bare concrete
scratching for crumbs of a taco,
I in the empty notebook,
cover titled, "I've Got This,"
seeking words slow to evolve.
I watch people arrive
and depart, unloading baskets,
desperate for food
denied conversation in the aisles,
frowning behind Lone Ranger masks.

More dogs arrive and I ask myself
why do masked consumers
bring their pets to grocery lots
to voice their outrage
at people sitting in cars
safely muffled, looking grim?

Most arrivals look past
"new low prices on produce
at 99 cents" signs,
locks click on car doors
against invasion by thieves.
Diseased strangers,
chosen family members
sent forth to pack
empty baskets on wheels,
hunters and gatherers filling,
then emptying them again,
leaving behind wire skeletons
waiting for newcomers
to the ground of unclaimed virus.

BIG GRAY CAT

The television yap, yap, yaps,
just and unjust vying for moments
in America's big screen politics.
Departing governance vows vengeance,
mudslinging, arms-bearing
polyglot of protesters gather,
audition for America's big screen politics.

I sit at my desk reading e. e. cummings
when a fat gray cat comes to my window,
tells me to view his offering
left in my backyard,
something he thinks as valuable as anything
remaining in this vast sandbox:
America's big screen politics.

ROMANCING CARDINALS

I thought they had deserted the yard
after chasing each other yesterday,
thought my looking on had alerted them,
a human peeping Tom
causing scurry for cover
in clumps of ginger.

Was it the wind shaking
leaves of sunlit bush
or passion flaunting
St. Francis's stony face?
The birds singing to each other
of good fortune coming

despite cats prowling the swept patio.
I believe they were sharing insights
about the nature of lasting love
among their feathered friends,
even among distrusting humans
seeing through a smudged pane
their one-time only nest.

BIRDS OF A FEATHER
(Or Farewell Donald Trump
7 a.m., Jan. 20, 2021)

A mockingbird lands in the bird bath
empty of water,
practices *noblesse oblige*
like the departing president
dirties the bowl,
drinks from his own pool,

shakes off his broken wings
and the powers of a sun king.
The world chants goodbye, strutting bird,
your soul long departed,
shrieking final thoughts
no one hears, no longer heeds.

POST INAUGURATION

From euphoria to ground
the day following inauguration;
grey clouds scatter.
The mind, clouded now, asks
where do we go from here?

Watching the leaves fall—
a south wind's prey—
one lonely rock
anchors itself
in the roots of a gnarled oak.

It was one line away from real,
a rhetoric heavily touted yesterday;
was it your first creative wave
or campaign poetry
placed in a drawer of the oval office?

She could have said,
be the poetry,
it was not meant to be
the mouth of politics,
but she wants to be president,

campaign for office,
lyrics hidden under heaped leaves
a few years hence
blown back into the face.

of an older language: Truth.

TO A KNOWN COPYIST

Like a rain drop
skittering on the surface
of a vast lake
you write three lines,
thinking the water has deepened.
But you are drowned in ego.
Go and sit with Basho,
wade at least 20 more years
in water beyond face level,
then write one true line.*

*With apologies to Ernest Hemingway, who wanted
to write one true sentence. And did.

SISTERS OF THE CLOTH
(News of a suicide)

What is this you brag about?
A friend's devotion taped
in heavy gift wrap —
bras, blue silk pajamas
sent to you, a professed nun?
You fold your arms
around her devotion
and smile betrayal.
She, a priest
unable to live as a discard
takes her own life.
The place in which she lives
not that of the perfect servant
dressed in a white collar
but floating in a black gown
of unrequited love,
palms turned upward
to the one who cherishes all.

WHILE READING CHARLES SIMIC

Privacy sleeps on clean white sheets,
secrecy, the home of bedbugs
and other sexual defilements
committed while reading
a book about exploiting trust,
an involved case if ever
there was a restless night
for everyone except
wandering lions
looking for a boulder
from which to spring
and collide with old shadows.

FLYING IN, FLYING OUT

Now and then grass appears,
false Spring's green shoots
rise among leaf mounds.
I think of all the green places
I've known and more of desert
tan and unyielding,
landscape unexpressed
where I seek surprises.
Here, robins as large as pigeons
land in an expanse like a park.
They look at me —
something alive but old fruit,
someone as unconversational
as the member of a Quakers meet,
no choice for a robin's meal,
nothing to sing about.

SACRIFICING EVERYTHING
TO BE IN LA-LA LAND

Oh, the body blow
an unruly adult child delivers,
this punch in my stomach,
breath wheezing out.
A daughter returns to addiction.
The chemical conqueror arrives.
In her disordered mind,
a frightened animal
grasps for shields against invasion
by those who love her.
She hunts for endangered shelter,
says there'll be a second chance…
oh yes — Repeat Dysfunction.

DRIED FLOWERS

When a camellia ages
it turns into a pink pansy,
at the least keeps color
on its cheeks.
Although the center darkens,
a reluctant owner, loath
to dispose of its innocent face
continues pouring water,
but no skeleton remains.
A flower remains a flower,
constancy in its heart,
beauty always beheld.

ZIPLINE

I've seen them in park sites,
lines stretching across air,
small boxes from which to launch,
a place unencumbered
until you push
your trembling body
into free expanse
and halfway down
make scissors of your legs,
whooping at nothingness
conquered with the something
of your glee,
landing on your feet.
With your history
a *fait accompli*.

WHAT YONDER SOUNDS

Morning air, drills in the street
just beyond our drive
pierce Consciousness,
pierce Unconsciousness.
A large machine
breaks concrete for reasons
only the neighbors know.
We were not warned.
The noise now absorbs
thought, an arrow
into the heart of any poems
waiting for birth, silenced
by some kind of progress,
the plumbing next door
constipated?
We hope it isn't pushed
into our drain,
enough already
on the surface of our lives.

THE POET MAXINE KUMIN

Consoled us in gardens,
flower and vegetable,
edible and inedible;
an invisible horsewoman
of unfailing humor
she now rides handsome steeds,
writes new legends.
Grace notes follow her
into the afterworld,
become imbedded in stained glass—
panes of red and purple,
poetry that takes us
above the glass,
above her well-turned gardens
into her wild heaven.

THE HEAT OF LOSS

Tragic news arrives,
a beloved friend terminally ill;
grief closes my throat,
memory closes my eyes:
Mah Jong at the Golf Club,
Khuzestan Province, 120 degrees,
Ahwaz, Iran, 1974.
She strides across the desert,
and I strain to keep up,
that brisk British walk
pulling me along.
We have set out for Ahwaz
after the game table,
too impatient to wait for taxis,
marbles of sweat
wets the long hair
we both once tended.
She runs out on the highway,
arms flailing the air,
a godsend, the Paykan taxi
spins toward us.
We begin to laugh,
red dog madness
that desert walk,
her laughter echoes
Ahwaz, Iran, 1974.
Grief closes my throat,
I try to let go.*

*Anne Saywell's death, 2021

AN ILL WIND THAT BLOWS

Yesterday, weak legs
unable to walk, listing left,
writing this to record
my body awry
or was it my brain?
I hate penning these lines,
no poetry
but disaster,
yet my handwriting sure
of all I learned in third grade
using a fountain pen
like this Parker,
pen all I know of fear,
always trying to write
a better ending.

II.

Tomato stew,
banana, blueberry,
coconut milkshake,
cure for whatever plagues me.
She smooths out the lumps,
taking care of by blending.
A doctor in disguise
she believes in natural healing
could have been
Christian Scientist
but Mary Baker Eddy
disapproves of any ingredient
save The Spirit
stirred into ethereal broth.
On Sunday as I rise
from a cushion
green and red stripes
shout save me,
balance disappears
as I grasp uncaring air,
fall into the arms
of my heroine
43 years and holding….

THIRTY-SEVEN DEGREES

And holding.
Louisiana weather
or an ice cap?
My limbs
and head
and toes, frozen.
Wind jostles Ginger plants.
Pools of night rain
flood the patio.
Inside I am wintry.
St. Francis hasn't moved,
is turning black
despite bird droppings
streaking his gown —
been on his feet too long.

A CHANGE OF APPETITE

Janis eats tortillas for breakfast,
Mexico comes to Alabama.
Her daughter marries a Gonzales.
She swings to a marimba,
all night music near Eufaula,
skirts swirling,
castanets clacking,
tosses her hair.
Ole' Janis,
the white flower falls
from long tresses
(she hates short hair).
She eats another tortilla,
shakes out her hair again.
A cloud of red dirt rises.

WHY WE WENT SOUTH

Snow at the foot of our oak
in the arch of its trunk,
winds out of northwest
blow hard on the study panes;
November we head South.
Never mind rain following snow
or ice beginning to sheet,
we do it every year
and pretend disbelief,
read that Florida basks
in 80 degrees shorts weather
and no need for caution.
In old Louisiana a cardinal,
wings iced over,
spirals into a nose dive,
skids into a pile of white leaves.

WHAT REALITY?

Easy to imagine
an alternative world,
one that ends in ice
rather than fire,
as Frost suggested;
easy to contemplate
white beards on heavy limbs
bent over
tired old men
soon to topple
without grace,
without humor,
looking older
than Our Father
and just as weary
of his look alikes.

SCREEN SAVER

Is that Big Sur
the majestic place
Balboa saw,
Monterey Pine
blowing awry
a cluster of red flowers
near rocks and cliffs
rising above the blue Pacific?
Home of giant kelp
and basking seals,
ecstasy captured
somewhere near Carmel,
somewhere mythic
and unforgettable
my screen renews daily.
My soul floats in tide pools.

BEN IN AUSTIN

Ben reads *Howl*
to a gang of caretakers
isolated in a Texas hotel,
minds fleeing to the road,
a group of incautious men
without destination
still in their pajamas.

THE DAY AFTER ASH WEDNESDAY

I keep looking at photos
in One Writer's Garden
where it lies on our coffee table;
Eudora Welty's love of beauty
inspires a garden
in our living room,
her camellias at home
on a multi-flowered Oriental rug.
In Jackson, Mississippi,
once warm in February,
Eudora would have declared
this ice and north wind
affronts to southern gardens,
so uninvited,
so out of season
for back porch company.

THE CHURCH POINT GARDEN IN WINTER

He brought in the pots,
leaves and blooms
luxuriant and cheerful,
no abiding in the out-of-doors.
But no one abiding indoors
without his plant life,
killer frosts and icy rain
now unable to unsettle greens
and pinks, reds and purples,
colors of his passion threatened
but never thwarted,
Darrell's eternal garden
growing under the veil of time.

OBESITY

Fat bodies,
something amiss,
appetite gone awry.
Frustration wants red meat,
thick dumplings,
gravy in a big black pot.
Each morsel
not a moment to savor
before turning to blubber,
topping for past unhappiness
undissolved by time.

CREATIVITY

I look through winter's dirty panes
at wilted Ginger fronds
compressing poems by cold;
if only thoughts could warm up
to lyrics not in the margins
but on long blue lines
at home on a yellow legal pad.

ORIGINALITY

I dislike copyists,
tamped down spirits
unable to suffer,
sissies about enduring
the pain of natural birth
to become original.

II.

I sit in an easy chair,
feet propped on brown hassock,
back stretched to heights
beyond my short stature,
enough to turn on
the lamp of creation
while looking at a thistle
under glass nearby,
sharp purple tentacles
needling my Unconscious.

BREAKFAST QUERY

It's a nagging question,
why do you write?
To feed the ego?
Or is there really a Muse
who sails in when the ego
is not at hand? In hand?

MENTOR

Did he really say,
"I love you
and everything that is in you:
poems, stories, place,
mind, imagination, spirit."
I can say the same of him.
No rights transferred.

THE PROVOCATION OF PANSIES

If you own two Parker pens and
write on a soft yellow tablet,
you may be a poet
who writes of yellow
and purple pansies
blooming in an earthen pot,
faces still upturned,
despite uncommon winter
claiming a welcome indiscretion.

THE RHINO WOMAN

Oh yes, flab jiggles
an invitation to a sick dance
accompanied by a fat tongue
prating deception.
Excess builds
layer by layer by layer
an accretion of lies.

TABLE TALK

Did father Harold teach me
admiration for trees and flowers?
Commanding at a querulous meal,
"Look at the trees."
Tall pines beyond the screen porch
absorb noise of quarreling,
now, the resin scent sifts through
a porous screen of time,
mealtime disturbance quelled
years hence.

A NEIGHBOR'S FENCE

The broken cypress fence
leans farther each day,
threatens a noisy fall.
But a Ginger tree nearby
resists its demise,
props up the weathered grey boards,
reminding me we are survivors.

SPRING?

Casualties of the winter storm:
a lizard yet partial green,
a dried earthworm
curled around itself.
I swept both away
along with my ambition
to write a blog
about casualties
of the winter storm
especially when a
lavender Japanese Magnolia
made a wry face at me.

COLORS

St. Francis's concrete gown
adapts to weather
from gray to black to green
like Joseph's many colored robe.
His message remains constant
among those amending colors:
be at peace.
Sun rise, sun set,
why fret about color?
Each day generously given
an invisible drama.

KAREN'S GLASS WORK

Cloudy glass in the sunroom
cannot obscure
Karen's happiness hangings:
stones, gems, a sky of glass,
the tree with broken limb.
How did she know
what I wanted to say
and cut it into being —
that mythic of my imagination?

GROCERY SHOPPING OR CAR SHOW?

In the parking lot again
sandwiched between vehicles,
I sit in the front seat of a Subaru
watching people I don't know
careful not to meet my eyes.
Food Mission, their avowed focus,
takes the latest model car,
the biggest SUV
to get a bag of groceries
they can hold in one hand
while making a sharp appraisal
of all shiny vehicles in the lot;
takes some theatrical talent
to open their elephantine trunks,
look around for an audience
and manage to appear hungry.

GREAT GRANDDAUGHTERS

The Romero twins in red velvet
and tiny gold shoes
flaunt a red bow
atop their long brown hair.
A Christmas wreath encircles
these beauties always on show.
Mama's dolls look wide-eyed,
benign but sassy at five,
are known to scream a favorite line
at their cowed father:
"How dare you?"
Chip off the old Mama.

IN ANOTHER PARKING LOT

A silver truck arrives at the pharmacy
and a chocolate Lab leaps from its bed;
Did he need a worm pill?
a rubber bone?
One command and he backs down,
climbs on the pick-up's tool box
and puts his head on his paws.
I wonder how any beautiful creature
learns how to be so gently obedient
from masters of practiced mendacity.

THE FINISH LINE

A toast to Henry Miller,
Charles Bukowski
and all free spirits
who wrote In the margins;
drew, painted,
rejected the world of jobs,
went about the real business
of living in the margins
because that is where
the artist's Self lives
in the true realm of joy
and dies a noble example —
if only as a footnote.

ABOUT THE AUTHOR:

Diane Marquart Moore is a poet, journalist, book author, and regular blogger at *A Word's Worth*, who divides her time between Sewanee, Tennessee, and New Iberia, Louisiana. She is a regular contributor to the *Pinyon Review*, a journal of Pinyon Publishing in Montrose, Colorado, has published in *The Southwestern Review* at the University of Louisiana, Lafayette, Louisiana, *Interdisciplinary Humanities*, *The Xavier Review*, *Acadiana Profile Magazine*, *American Weave*, *Louisiana Historical Review*, *Trace*, and other literary journals. She has been an associate editor for *Acadiana Lifestyle Magazine*, New Iberia, Louisiana, feature writer and columnist for *The Daily Iberian*, New Iberia, Louisiana, as well as a feature writer and book reviewer for *The Yaddasht Haftegy* in Ahwaz, Iran where she lived during the reign of the Shahanshah. Her young adult book, *Martin's Quest*, was a finalist in the Heekins Foundation Award Contest and was selected to be on the supplementary reading list for gifted and talented students by the Louisiana Library Association. Heron Press received a grant from the Gheens Foundation of Louisiana to provide *Martin's Quest* as a supplementary text for middle-grade and high school students in Lafourche and Terrebonne parishes during the book's publication year. Moore has written 955 posts and received 283,883 pages of views on her blog, *A Word's Worth*. She is a retired archdeacon of the Episcopal Diocese of Western Louisiana.

BY DIANE MARQUART MOORE

POETRY
Ridges
iDoodle
We Vagabonds
An Ordinary Day
Field Marks
Consolation of Gardens
Ultimate Pursuit
All Love,
Let the Trees Answer
Spring's Kiss
Above the Prairie
Sifting Red Dirt
A Slow-Moving Stream
Street Sketches
Corner of Birch Street
Strand of Beads
A Lonely Grandmother
Between Plants and Humans
Night Offices
Departures
In a Convent Garden
Mystical Forest
Everything is Blue
Post Cards from Diddy Wah Diddy
Alchemy
Old Ridges
Rising Water

The Holy Present and Farda
Grandma's Good War
Afternoons in Oaxaca (Las Poesias)
The Book of Uncommon Poetry
Counterpoint
Your Chin Doesn't Want to Marry
Soaring
More Crows
Just Passing Through
Moment Seized

YOUNG ADULTS
Martin and the Last Tribe
Martin Finds His Totem
Flood on the Rio Teche
Sophie's Sojourn in Persia
Kajun Kween
Martin's Quest

ADULT FICTION
Redeemed by Blood
Silence Never Betrays
Chant of Death with Isabel Anders
Goat Man Murder
The Maine Event
Nothing for Free

CHILDREN
The Beast Beelzebufo
The Cajun Express

NON-FICTION
Porch Posts with Janet Faulk-Gonzales
Iran: In A Persian Market
Their Adventurous Will
Live Oak Gardens
Treasures of Avery Island

We hope you enjoyed reading this Border Press book.

In the Margins is the last book Diane wrote before her death on September 2, 2021. Her blog at "A Word's Worth" (revmoore.blogspot.com) can still be viewed. If you would like to read more books and ebooks by Diane Marquart Moore and subscribe to our mailing list, send email to victoria@borderpress-books.com.

To learn about books in other genres published by Border Press Books, go to the website at www.borderpressbooks.com. In addition, you may order our books at Amazon.com.